HAVE YOU SEEN THE ARBAʿEEN?

Dr. Heussane

Copyright © 2024 Dr. Heussane

All rights reserved.

ISBN: 9798992001617

www.DrHeussane.com

On the day of ʿAshura, the 10th day of Muharram, the bad guys did something so bad. Imam Husayn's [Peace be upon him] horse came back without him. So the women and children knew what had happened to him and the other good guys. They were so sad. But they were patient.

Despite their sadness, they knew the real winner of this fight. The true winners are those who decide to do what is right.

The bad guys set fire to the family's tents. The women and children had to run for their lives.

Why did they burn the tents of Imam Husayn^(Peace be upon him) when he died? Maybe they wanted the kids to be afraid when they cried.

They hurt the ladies and the kids. They stole their things. The family really missed Imam Husayn.[Peace be upon him]

If 'Abbas[Peace be upon him] were still here the bad guys would not dare touch them. Even though these were the Prophet's[Peace be upon him & his progeny] relatives, they hurt them.

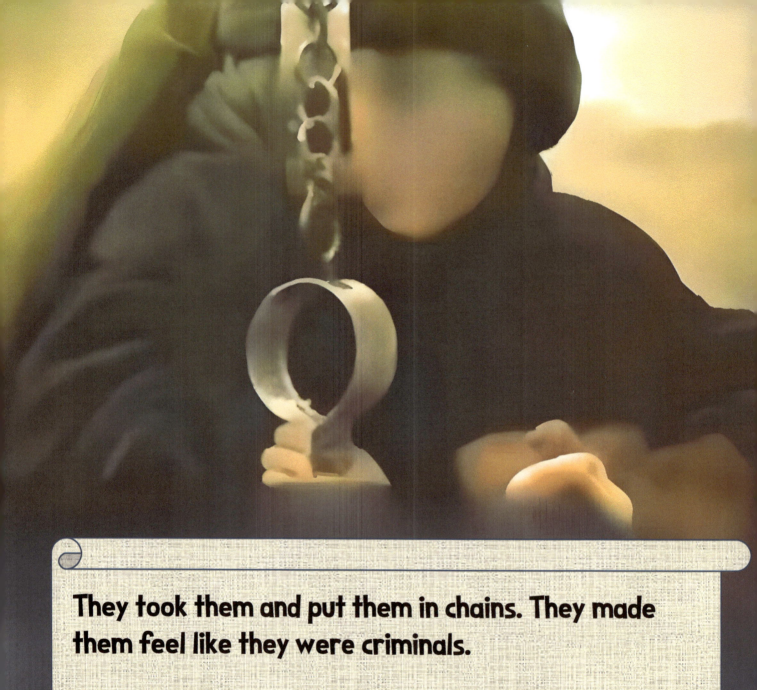

They took them and put them in chains. They made them feel like they were criminals.

Imagine seeing a young girl hugging her brave mother.
Even if mommy was scared, she loved her and her brother.

They had to leave Imam Husayn's (Peace be upon him) blessed body in Karbala (the holy land of) without a proper burial. They had to leave their beloved martyrs under the scorching Sun.

Fighting should be the last resort, for patience is true might. Martyrs are those who are killed while fighting for what is right.

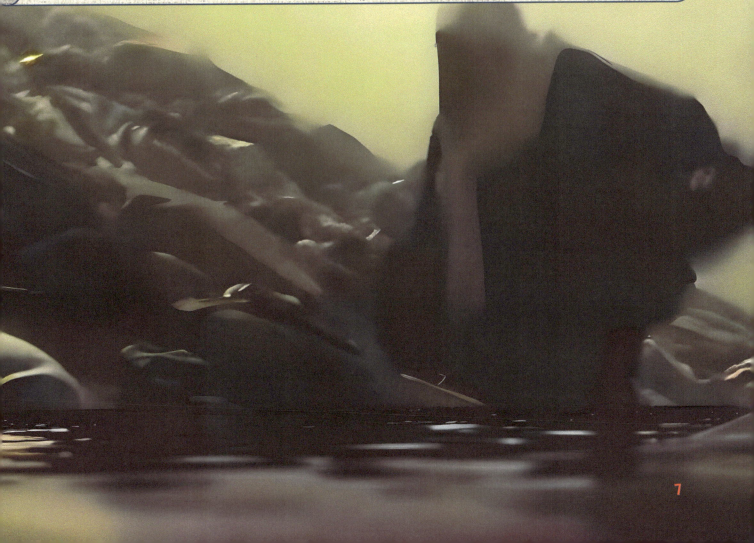

The bad guys held the blessed head of Imam Husayn^(Peace be upon him) on top of a spear as if it were a trophy. Their hearts had become so dark because of their bad deeds.

See the children walking in the desert with their mothers. They call them orphans now after the death of their fathers.

They took the family of Imam Husayn[Peace be upon him] to the bad guy leader in Kufa. He tried to blame God, Allah[The Almighty], for the bad deeds of his army.

The Creator makes life and gives us the choice to choose well. Care for this gift or break it, you choose your heaven or hell.

He threatened to kill Imam ʿAli Zayn al-ʿAbideen *(Peace be upon him)* because he spoke the truth. But Lady Zaynab *(Peace be upon her)*, Imam Husayn's *(Peace be upon him)* sister, defended her nephew *(Peace be upon him)*, who was so ill.

"Then kill me with him!" she *(Peace be upon her)* would exclaim, shocking the bad guy. But all learned that the true Imam *(Peace be upon him)* was not afraid to die.

Imam Zayn al-ʿAbideen *(Peace be upon him)* was not killed then, he was imprisoned. But they say Allah *(The Almighty)* helped him go to bury Imam Husayn's *(Peace be upon him)* blessed body 3 days after ʿAshura.

To Karbala *(the holy land of)* and back, by God's *(The Almighty)* permission, they would say.
True Imams *(Peace be upon them)* care for their burial in a special way.

The blessed bodies were buried. But the journey of the women and children was just beginning. The evil-doers forced them to go from place to place.

They wanted people to be afraid to do what is right.
But God (The Almighty) has a rescue plan to help people see the light.

The bad guys made the women and children go from place to place for many days. They were hurting them so much. They did not respect them.

Noble ladies should be treated like the queens that they are. Respect their privacy up close and even from afar.

They arrived to Damascus and were taken to the worst bad guy there, Yazeed. He used his stick to hit Imam Husayn's *Peace be upon him* blessed head. So disrespectful, so evil!

Yazeed would say things that hinted why he chose to do this. To get back at the Prophet, *Peace be upon him & his progeny* hitting the face he would kiss.

14

The good people were sad. Some were scared. Some were angry. They loved Imam Husayn^(Peace be upon him) because Prophet Muhammad^(Peace be upon him & his progeny) loved him.

This evil would break the Prophet's^(Peace be upon him & his progeny) heart—so one man would say. But Yazeed said he wanted the man kicked out right away!

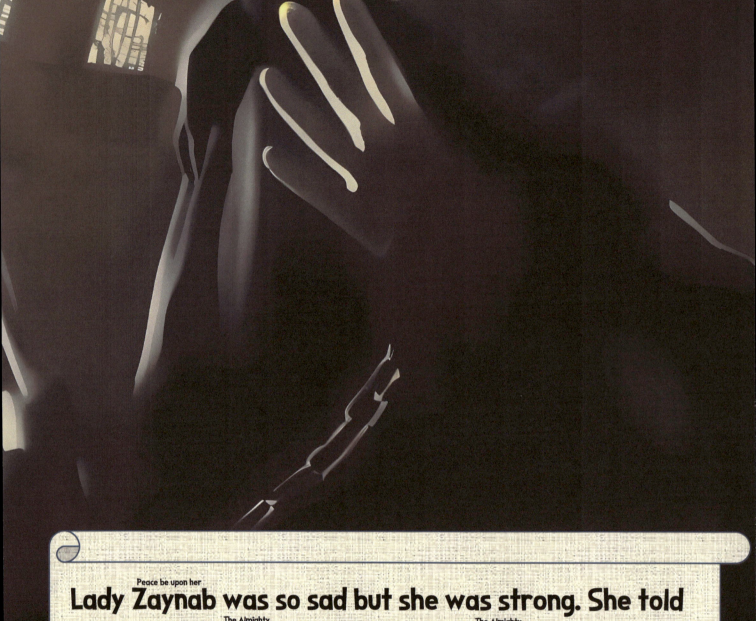

Lady Zaynab (Peace be upon her) was so sad but she was strong. She told Yazeed that Allah (The Almighty) is watching him. Allah (The Almighty) does not love when you hurt the good guys. God (The Almighty) will fix this one day.

Only a few days are left—get ready to face your fate! God (The Almighty) is fair, so cut your losses before it is too late.

Imam Zayn al-ʿAbideen [Peace be upon him] told the people who they were: O' people, these are the good guys. Yazeed is fighting against the best people.

We grew up learning from the best [Peace be upon them], loving to pray and give. My home was the best school, my town was the best place to live.

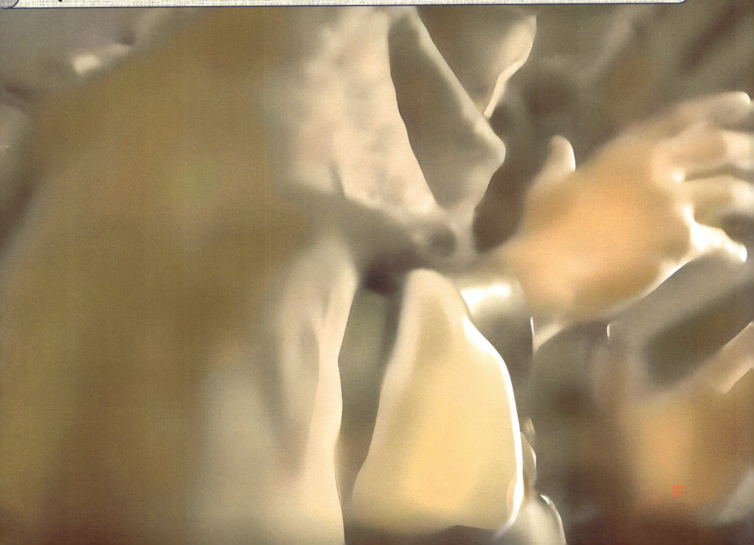

The good Imam[Peace be upon him] **explained until it became clear. Many started to cry because they now knew what really happened. Yazeed decided to send them home.**

Yazeed would fear that the tears wake people up and cause war. So he would send them back and try to trick people some more.

They say that on the way back to Medina, the family stopped to visit the martyrs in Karbala. It would be 40 days after ʿAshura—the "Arbaʿeen day visit."

At the graves of their heroes, they would remember that scene. This would mark the very first "Ziyara of Arbaʿeen."

The women and children sat at the graves of their loved ones. They would remember ᶜAbbas^(Peace be upon him) and how the bad guys hurt both of his hands.

^(Peace be upon him) ᶜAbbas was killed while trying to get the children some water. Wisely holding the flag, protecting sister as daughter.

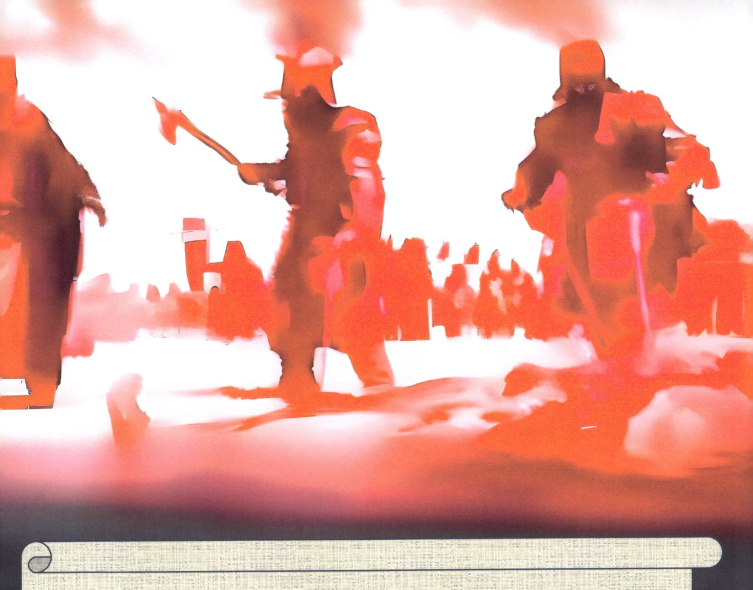

The memories of what happened and the stories they heard were so heartbreaking. They would feel that the sky and the land were sad too.

It is no surprise if the sky cried to God^(The Almighty) about it.
All things might have a way to speak, though we may not know it.

21

Today, those who love Imam Husayn [Peace be upon him] still visit his shrine in [the holy city of] Karbala. The visit of Arbaʿeen, 40 days after ʿAshura, on the 20th of Safar, is a special sign.

Thousands of thousands, millions, walk from [the holy city of] Najaf to this place. "We are here for you [Peace be upon you], Husayn," echoes across time and space.

Some come from even farther away, but many walk from Najaf (the holy city of) to Karbala (the holy city of). On the way, there are places to rest. Many love to help these special guests.

Hungry? Thirsty? Tired? They would love to serve you for free. Because they love Imam Husayn (Peace be upon him), whom you have come to see.

There are 1452 poles on the way between Najaf (the holy city of) and Karbala (the holy city of) today. There are about 50 meters between each two poles. At pole 1452, the shrine is very close.

Start from Imam Ali's (Peace be upon him) grave in Najaf (the holy city of) at pole number one. Then head to Karbala (the holy city of)—visit Imam Husayn, his son. (Peace be upon them)

Imagine we have reached pole 313. That is 100 + 100 + 100 + 10 + 3 = 313. What is next? 314, 315, 316, 317…

Stop for a bit—think of the number three hundred thirteen. Discuss its meaning, now and during the Arbaʿeen.

The love of Imam Husayn ^(Peace be upon him) makes them want to walk more. Even when they are tired, they rest so that they can walk some more.

On foot or in wheelchairs, they learn to help one another.
Of all colors and cultures, this love brings them together.

Now imagine we have reached pole 1452. that is 1000 + 400 + 50 + 2 = 1452. What is next? The shrine is up ahead!

We are here for you today, whether in sunshine or rain. With loving hearts and little hands, labbayka ya Husayn!

We will never leave you, O'
Peace be upon you
Husayn!

The Almighty
Thank God for this gift! The
Peace be upon him
love of Husayn...

Have you seen the Arba`een? The walk of love during the day and through the night.

Despite my sadness, I know the real winner of this fight. The true winners are those who decide to do what is right.

Milton Keynes UK
Ingram Content Group UK Ltd.
UKHW050232021224
451791UK00009B/46